Why Did Grandpa Die?

A Book About Death

By Barbara Shook Hazen

Illustrated by Pat Schories

*Prepared with the cooperation of Bernice Berk, Ph.D., of
The Bank Street College of Education.*

A GOLDEN BOOK • NEW YORK
Western Publishing Company, Inc.   Racine, Wisconsin 53404

Note to Parents

Children need to know the true facts about death. They are less afraid when they do. The death of someone they know will raise many questions and worries. Since children are very literal, anything but an honest answer to their questions can be very confusing and upsetting. A family's religious beliefs may help parents frame answers as well, but the basic facts about death must be presented.

Here are some dos and don'ts about talking with your children about death.

Don't say the person "went away." The child may feel abandoned, or think he or she did something wrong and is no longer loved.

Don't say death is the same as sleep. The child might become afraid of going to sleep himself.

Don't say that being sick causes death. Even if a sickness *did* lead to the death, you must be very careful to explain the difference between a fatal illness and a simple one which can be treated and cured.

Do let a child attend the funeral or other services if he wants to. Children should be allowed to express their grief with other members of the family. Seeing that everyone feels sad helps the child deal with his own feelings.

Do tell your child that it is okay to feel sad and cry. It's much better to express feelings of sadness. That helps to make a death more manageable for children—and adults.

Do try and prepare the child ahead of time, if possible, so he can understand what's happening. For example, if a pet dies, discuss what that means. Discuss the different life spans of animals and humans, talk about how the leaves change in the fall, or describe how plants grow in the spring and die in the winter.

Do help your child remember all the wonderful things he can about the person who has died. Memory is the lasting link that can help children and adults accept a death.

WHY DID GRANDPA DIE? helps parents open discussion with their children at a very difficult time. Reading this book to a child is a way to help the child share his or her feelings, and discover that the comfort people can bring to each other is very helpful—and very necessary.

—The Editors

When Molly was a baby, everyone said she took after Grandpa. She had his dimples, his curly hair, and his curiosity.

And she gave him her first smile.

As Molly grew older, she and Grandpa grew closer. He took her to the park, and taught her how to sail a boat.

Afterwards, he always made pink lemonade his special way.

Everyone said Molly and Grandpa were alike as two peas in a pod.

They both liked mushed ice cream, wildflowers, and woodsy walks.

They both didn't like big ocean waves, lima beans, and being told to hurry.

One day, Molly and Grandpa planted a wildflower garden by the back fence. Grandpa showed Molly how to prepare the ground, and plant the seeds, and put down markers.

While planting, Molly found a dead butterfly.

"Look, Grandpa. He isn't moving," said Molly.

"He won't move or fly ever again," said Grandpa.

They buried the butterfly in the soft ground, and put a pretty egg-shaped stone on top to mark the place.

"How can he breathe under the ground?" Molly asked.

"He's dead now. He doesn't breathe," said Grandpa. "But it is nice to remember how he was when he was alive."

The next day Grandpa was going to take Molly sailing
in a real boat as an early birthday treat.
But Grandpa didn't feel well.
His chest hurt and he had trouble catching his breath.
He whispered he would take Molly another day.

"But you promised," said Molly. "I want to go now."
"Yes, I know," said Grandpa. "But I don't feel up to it."
"Molly," her mother said sharply, "don't pester Grandpa."
"Okay, okay," said Molly, even though it wasn't okay. Molly was angry because Grandpa broke his promise to her.

The day after that, Grandpa went to a hospital.
As he left, he told Molly, "Don't worry, they're going
to fix me up just fine. We'll go sailing when I get back."
"Okay," said Molly, giving Grandpa a get-well kiss.

But Grandpa didn't get better. Instead, he got sicker.
Now, a lot of the time, Molly's mother acted cross and
her father was sad. Now, Molly played in her room a lot.

Then one day the phone rang and Molly heard her
mother say, "Oh, no," in a funny voice.

Molly wanted to ask what was wrong. But she didn't
because she was scared it was about something bad, and
maybe it was about something bad she had done.

Molly's father came home right away. He hugged
Molly hard and said, "Grandpa is gone."

"Where'd he go?" asked Molly. "And why didn't he take
me?"

"Grandpa is dead," Molly's father said.

"He can't be dead," said Molly. "He said they'd fix him up just fine."

"He was old and very ill and couldn't be fixed up, even with good care," Molly's father said. Then he held Molly tighter and started to cry.

Molly was upset and wriggled away. She ran to her room and lay on her bed.

She felt empty and awful and frightened. But she didn't feel like crying.

Soon Molly's father came in. He sat on the edge of the bed and said, "Grandpa was my father and I loved him very much. I know you loved him very much, too. And he loved you very, very much."

"Then why did Grandpa have to go and die?" asked Molly.

"Everything that lives has to die, someday," said Molly's father softly. "Death is the end of life."

Molly threw her panda pillow. "But he promised me we'd go sailing. It isn't fair."

Molly's mother came in later with some pink
lemonade.

"I don't want it the way you make it," Molly said. "I
want Grandpa."

"So do I, and so does your father," said Molly's mother.
"But he's dead and we can't see him again, except in
pictures and in memories."

"But I don't want him to be dead," said Molly, turning
away.

A few days later, there was a funeral service for Grandpa. Everybody said nice things about him.

But the service was long and the day was hot, and Molly felt wriggly. Some grown-ups cried a lot, as if they couldn't stop, and that scared Molly.

After the service, everybody went to the graveyard.
There were lots of flowers there, but not the wild kind
Grandpa liked.

While more talking was going on, Molly picked some
daisies. She put them in a bunch by the other flowers,
and said, "Good-bye, Grandpa."

But she still had the feeling he would be back.

The feeling gradually grew less, but Molly still missed Grandpa a lot.

She missed him when the leaves fell, and he wasn't there to giggle and kick the leaves with her.

She missed him when her birthday came and there was no special pink lemonade, and no present from Grandpa with a smile face instead of an ordinary card.

She missed Grandpa when school started, because lots of the time he used to take her.

When it was her turn to tell "What I Did Last Summer," Molly talked the whole time about Grandpa, about what they did, and how he died.

When she talked about it, it seemed more real.

That night Molly cried for the first time in a long time. Her mother held her close and cried too, and said, "Tears help you let out your sad feelings and then you can begin to feel better."

By the time summer came again, Molly still missed
Grandpa. But she didn't feel sad every time she thought
of him.

Now the garden she and Grandpa planted was in
bloom. "I wish he could see it," Molly told her mother
while they were picking flowers.

"The garden is a nice present Grandpa left for us," said
Molly's mother. "And it helps us remember him."

Now, Molly understood at last that Grandpa would not be back, ever.

But she still talked to him sometimes, in the garden, which had been their special place.

"I talk to him because I still like to tell him things, even if he can't hear," Molly told her father one day when they were weeding.

Later that summer, when Molly's cousins came to visit, Molly showed them the garden. She told them Grandpa stories, and made them pink lemonade just the way Grandpa did it.

"He's dead," Molly told them. "I'll never kiss him again, or go places with him again. But I'll remember him—always."

And Molly always did remember Grandpa, all the long
while she was growing up and going on to new things.
And she remembered him long after she was grown,
and had children of her own who loved Grandpa's pink
lemonade, and Grandpa's stories, and a house full of
flowers.